Balboa Press books may be ordered through booksellers or by contacting:

Balboa Press
A Division of Hay House
1663 Liberty Drive
Bloomington, IN 47403
www.balboapress.com
844-682-1282

Because of the dynamic nature of the Internet, any web addresses or links contained in this book may have changed since publication and may no longer be valid. The views expressed in this work are solely those of the author and do not necessarily reflect the views of the publisher, and the publisher hereby disclaims any responsibility for them.

Any people depicted in stock imagery provided by Getty Images are models, and such images are being used for illustrative purposes only.
Certain stock imagery © Getty Images.

ISBN: 978-1-5043-6875-9 (sc)
ISBN: 978-1-5043-6876-6 (e)

Library of Congress Control Number: 2016917850

Print information available on the last page.

Balboa Press rev. date: 10/12/2020

Dedication

This book is dedicated to

Elizabeth

As a little child I come to earth,
to learn about the world and its ways.

I am excited to be here with family and friends
expressing God's love every day.

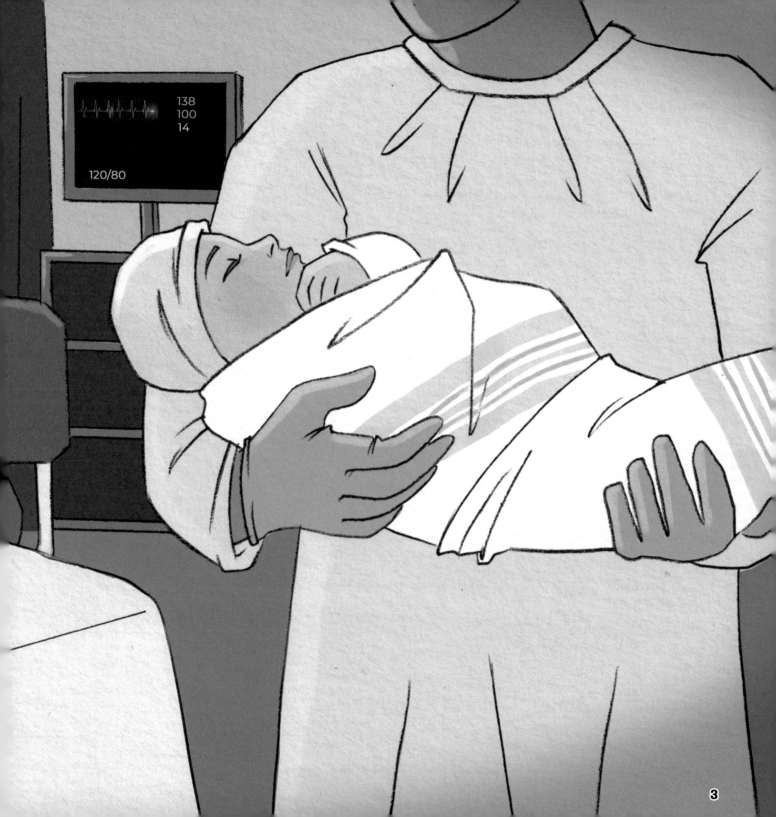

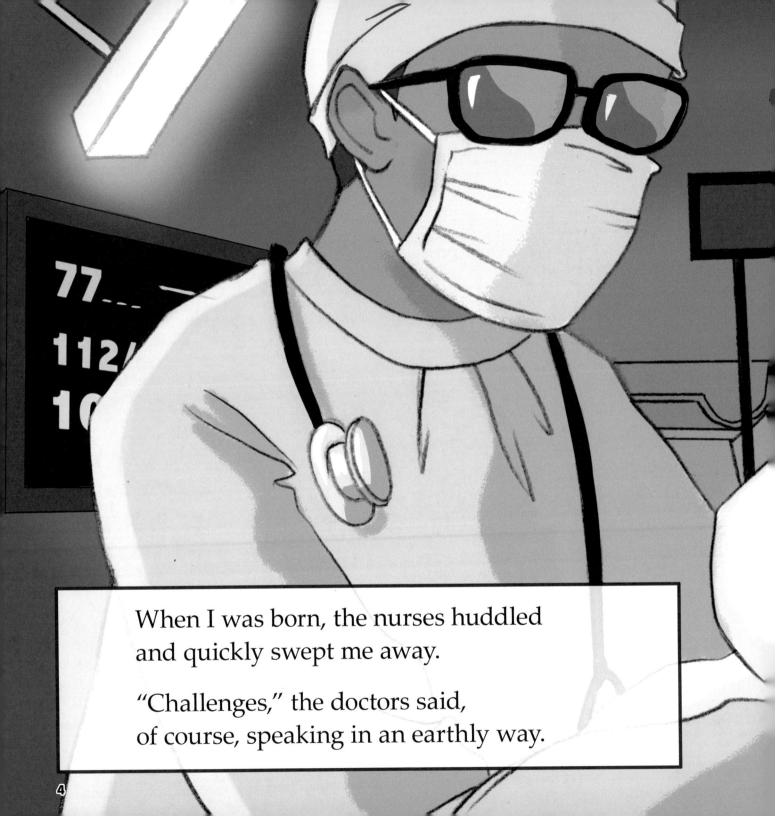

When I was born, the nurses huddled
and quickly swept me away.

"Challenges," the doctors said,
of course, speaking in an earthly way.

4

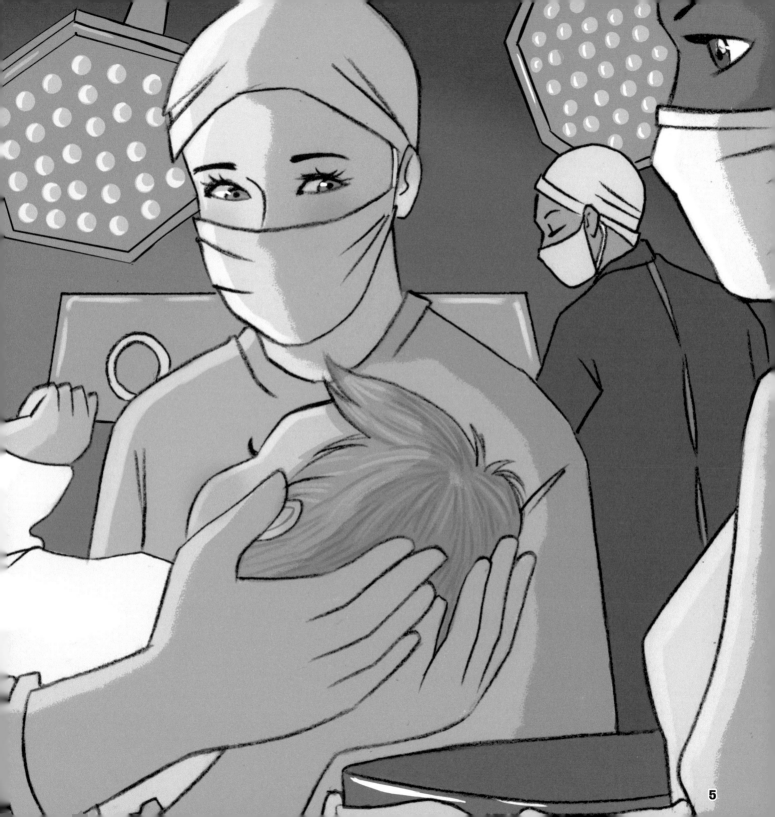

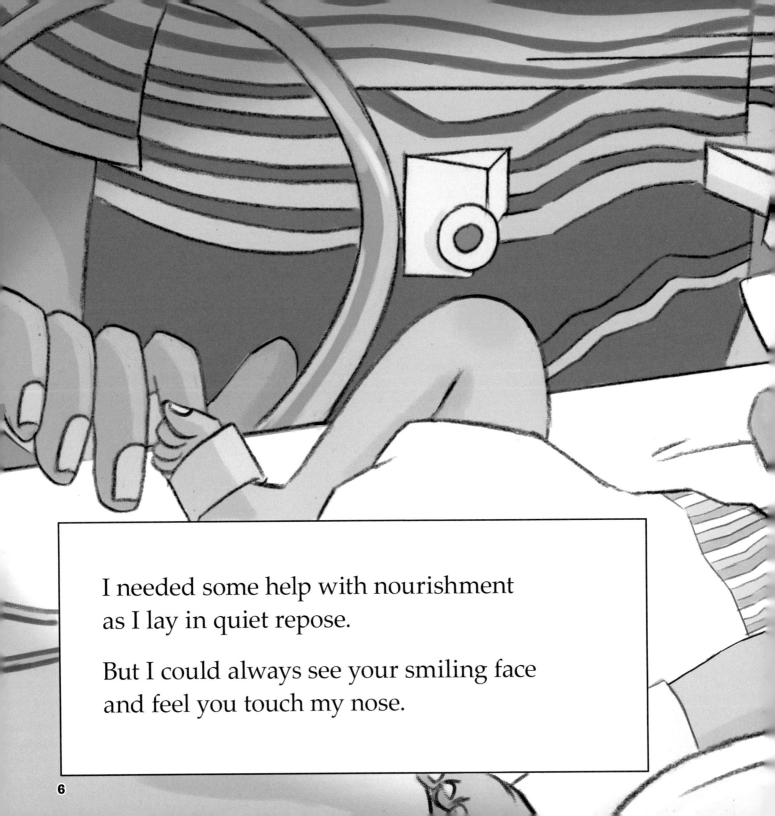

I needed some help with nourishment
as I lay in quiet repose.

But I could always see your smiling face
and feel you touch my nose.

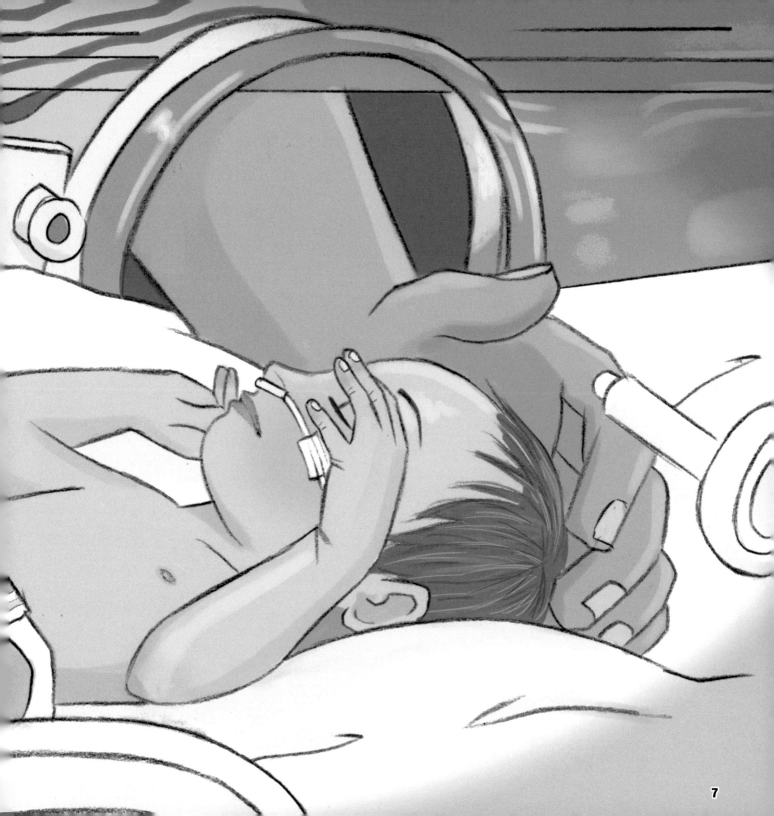

As I have grown and learned to adjust
to life on this earthly plane,

I think of you and remember your care
and acknowledge the times of pain.

It's a challenge to watch others climb on the playground,
as I patiently wait at the side.

While others call out to play with friends,
I would love to go down the slide.

11

No matter the challenges…
I feel God's love within me, each moment of each day.
And because of His love and comfort, I just want to say…

I may not be able to run and play,
but, if I could, I'd climb mountains to honor His ways.

I may not be able to speak words clearly, but
I'll speak through my actions as I love Him dearly.

I may not be able to jump and spin,
but I can express His love from within.

I may not be able to read His words
or expound upon His writings,

But I listen and feel His Love coming through
and my heart feels so delighted.

Please don't just see my challenges.
I am truly differently abled.

I am much more than the words
by which I am officially labeled.

Look into my heart and know
the love of God is what you're seeing.

As it is inside of every human being…

Look into my heart and know…
So below as it is above.

See only love…

See Only Love

Inspiration

My daughter is a Physical Therapist. In fact, she has her doctorate in Physical Therapy. She chooses to work in a school district as the physical therapist who services the Individual Education Plans for children with disabilities.

As I have watched her over the years, I am in awe and have great respect for her and for the children and adults that she serves.

No matter where we are, these children and young people (and their families) "turn inside out" to communicate with her and receive her attention. She smiles and talks and laughs with them, acknowledging them and loving them.

She would always say that she wished she could "take them home." I have thought, so many times, how lucky they were to have a therapist who loved them so much.

Elizabeth participates in many volunteer activities with these differently abled individuals. These activities include Special Olympics, Sailing, Ice Skating, Swimming, Horseback Riding, and she started a Cheerleading Squad for the differently abled. They go to several performance activities where Cheerleading Squads are competing. This special Cheer Squad is always warmly received.

What wonderful emissaries of Light and Love! They do their routines out of pure joy! The attendees and other able-bodied cheer squads watch their routines and they can see this special Cheer Squad's pure love of participation and the experience.

At the ice skating show they come out with helpers who guide their apparatus and support them, but the joy is apparent as they glide and slide on the ice. As we watch and clap in approval, several participants stop on the ice and look into the audience and wave and wave and wave. We all wave back, tears running down our cheeks, acknowledging the pure joy and the love they are expressing. Through the tears we know God's spirit is within each person and expressed in a variety of ways. God has a plan for each of us and asks us only to *see* love, to *be* love and to *express* Love.

Through our heartfelt tears, we see a kaleidoscope of color. The Light of God shining through each of us, like a kaleidoscope of color in all of its beauty, shining forth in love and acceptance, showing the way back to Love… to Source.

Our lives would lack this special beauty if we were all the same. We move forward in embracing our differences as we are challenged to *See Only Love.*

Author: Marian S. Taylor

Marian S. Taylor, EdD, is a retired university professor. Her career began at the elementary level where she taught first grade and served as a reading specialist. She was director of the university laboratory school and a chairperson of a university department. She taught undergraduate and graduate classes while at the university and spent many years directing the program for the development of reading specialists.

Marian has been very involved with her family and with church activities. She is the mother of three grown children and is very proud of her grandchildren. Other publications can be viewed at www.marianstaylor.com

Illustrator: Amy Duarte

Amy Duarte began her career as an artist working for Walt Disney Animation Studios. From there, she leapt into the world of visual effects and graphic arts on more than 30 feature films like "Pirates of the Caribbean: At World's End," "The Amazing Spiderman," "Mr. and Mrs. Smith," etc. She was appointed as a lead artist for several major motion pictures, including "Fantastic Four," where she advised and guided a team of artists on creating the special effects of Jessica Alba's character (Sue Storm).

Born in Jakarta, Indonesia, and raised in three different countries, Amy is fluent in six languages and an avid polo player. She was also on the design team that created the top secret commercial for Apple's Watch before the product was launched. Her portfolio can be viewed at www.amyduarte.com.

Printed in the United States
By Bookmasters